Life Cycle of a
Sunflower

Angela Royston

Heinemann Library
Des Plaines, Illinois

Designed by Celia Floyd
Illustrations by Alan Fraser
Printed in Hong Kong / China

02 01 00 99
10 9 8 7 6 5 4 3 2 1

The Library of Congress has cataloged the hardcover version of this book as follows:

Library of Congress Cataloging-in-Publication Data

Royston, Angela.
 Life cycle of a sunflower / by Angela Royston.
  p. cm.
 Includes bibliographical references and index.
 Summary: Introduces the parts, pollination, life cycle, and farming of sunflowers.
  ISBN 1-57572-699-8 (lib. bdg.)
  1. Sunflowers--Life cycles--Juvenile literature.
 [1. Sunflowers.] I. Title
 SB299.S9R69 1998
 583'.99--dc21   98-10733
                                                                      CIP
                                                                       AC

Paperback ISBN 1-57572-475-8

Acknowledgments
The Publisher would like to thank the following for permission to reproduce photographs: A–Z Botanical Collection/Joyce Hammond p.14; Bruce Coleman/S Nielsen p. 11; FLPA/Gerard Lacz p. 18; Harry Smith Collection p. 20; Holt Studios International/Nigel Cattlin p. 5, 7, 8, 10, 15, 19, 21, 26-27; NHPA/A N T p. 16, NHPA/Roger Tidman p. 23, NHPA/Christophe Ratier p. 24, NHPA/K Ghani p. 25; Oxford Scientific/Stephen Downer p. 9, 12, 13, Oxford Scientific/Martyn Chillmaid p. 17, Oxford Scientific/Patti Murray p. 22; Roger Scruton p. 6; The Garden Picture Library/Chris Burrows p. 4.

Cover photograph: Tony Stone Images/Karen Smith.

Our thanks to Dr. John Feltwell, Wildlife Matters Consultancy, in the preparation of this edition.

Contents

What are Sunflowers?

Sunflowers are tall plants with large, flat flowers. They come from North America, but now grow in other parts of the world, too.

3 days   I week   6 weeks

There are many kinds of sunflowers, but the sunflower in this book has bright yellow petals. All sunflowers grow from large seeds.

8 weeks

10 weeks

13 weeks

Seeds

The seed is as big as your thumbnail.
It is planted in spring when the soil
is warm and damp. Inside is a tiny
plant which begins to grow.

3 days   1 week   6 weeks

The **roots** of the plant push down through the soil. They are covered in tiny hairs which take in water. A green **shoot** grows upwards.

8 weeks

10 weeks

13 weeks

Sprouting

1 to 2 weeks

The green **shoot** is sprouting through the soil. The first leaves open out. They use sunlight, air, and water to make food for the plant.

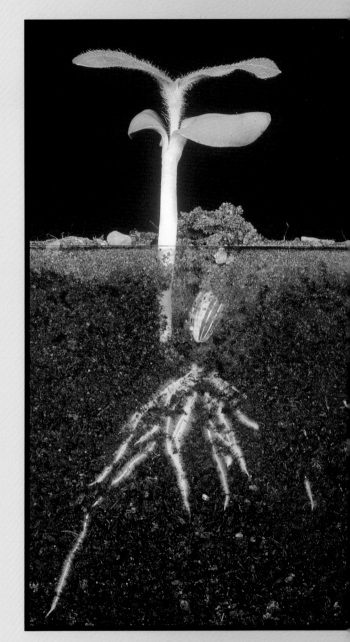

3 days

1 week

6 weeks

The plant grows taller and more leaves grow at the tip of the stem. The stem is covered with fine hairs to stop insects from climbing up it.

8 weeks

10 weeks

13 weeks

Growing   4 to 6 weeks

The leaves grow bigger. Under the ground the **roots** grow longer. They take in the water and **minerals** the plant needs to stay alive and keep growing.

3 days   I week   6 weeks

A large bud forms at the end of the stem. It is protected by pointed green **bracts** that look like small leaves.

Flowering   6 to 8 weeks

The **bracts** unfold and the bud begins to open.

3 days   1 week   6 weeks

Underneath the bracts are lots of yellow petals.

8 weeks

10 weeks

13 weeks

9 weeks

The plant grows taller and taller. The flowers open out. Each **flower head** is made up of many tiny flowers.

3 days

1 week

6 weeks

All the sunflowers turn to face the sun. As the sun moves across the sky, the flower heads turn to follow it.

8 weeks

10 weeks

13 weeks

16

Each **flower head** is made up of
hundreds of tiny flowers called
florets. The tips of these florets
are covered with a fine yellow dust
called **pollen**.

3 days

1 week

6 weeks

The flower head is growing bigger. Honey bees see the bright yellow petals and come to the flower head to collect pollen.

8 weeks

10 weeks

13 weeks

As the honey bee crawls across the **florets**, its body and legs become covered with **pollen**. The bee flies from one **flower head** to another.

3 days

1 week

6 weeks

Some of the pollen rubs off its body into the florets. In the center of each floret is a tiny **ovule**. The ovule becomes a seed when a grain of **pollen** joins it.

19

New Seeds

The **florets** have no **pollen** left, but inside each one a seed is beginning to swell. The petals around the **flower head** wilt and fall off.

3 days   I week   6 weeks

The flower heads become darker
and turn almost black. Some of
them are so heavy they droop from
the end of the stems.

The **florets** wither too. The **flower head** is now a flat disk of shiny black seeds.

3 days   1 week   6 weeks

Birds feed on the seeds. The birds drop some of the seeds as they fly away. These may grow into new plants next year.

8 weeks

10 weeks

13 weeks

Harvesting

The farmer has come to **harvest** the sunflower seeds. The harvester cuts the plants and shakes out the seeds.

3 days

1 week

6 weeks

The harvester missed this plant!
The leaves wither and die. Some of
the seeds that fall to the ground will
grow into new plants next spring.

8 weeks   10 weeks   13 weeks

A Field of Sunflowers

Farmers grow sunflowers for their seeds. Most of the seeds are crushed and made into animal feed or squeezed to make sunflower oil.

Some seeds are roasted for us to eat as snacks. Pet guinea pigs like to eat sunflower seeds, too. Some seeds are kept to be planted next spring.

Life Cycle

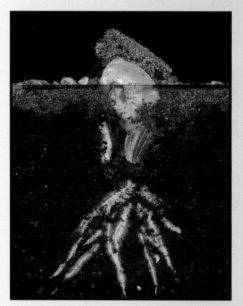

1 Sprouting

2 Sprouting

3

Flowering

Flowering

4

Pollination

5

New Seeds

6

Fact File

Sunflowers can grow taller than a one-floor house.

The **flower head** can be as big as a dinner plate.

Each flower head may produce 1,000 seeds. Most seeds are made into oil and margarine.

Sunflowers grow all over the world but more are grown in Russia than in any other country.

Glossary

bracts parts of a plant that protect the bud while it grows. In most other kinds of flowers they are called sepals

floret a tiny flower which is part of a **flower head**

flower head a flower that is made up of many tiny **florets**

harvest to gather ripe crops

nutrients plant food in the soil that the plant needs to grow and stay healthy

ovule female egg that forms a seed when joined by a male pollen grain

pollen the tiny male seeds of a plant that look like yellow dust

roots the parts of a plant that grow under the ground, take in water and hold the plant up

shoot the first stem and leaves of a new plant

More Books to Read

Legg, Gerald. *From Seed to Sunflower.* Danbury, CT: Franklin Watts, 1998.

Prevost, John F. *Sunflowers.* Minneapolis, MN: Abdo & Daughters Publishing, 1996.

Winner, Cherie. *The Sunflower Family.* Minneapolis, MN: Lerner Publishing, 1996.

Index